EASY PIANO
LEVEL 3–4

Holiday Songs & Christmas Carols

Arranged by RICHARD BRADLEY

Richard Bradley is one of the world's best-known and best-selling arrangers of piano music for print. His success can be attributed to years of experience as a teacher and his understanding of students' and players' needs. His innovative piano methods for adults (Bradley's How to Play Piano – Adult Books 1, 2, and 3) and kids (Bradley for Kids – Red, Blue, and Green Series) not only teach the instrument, but they also teach musicianship each step of the way.

Originally from the Chicago area, Richard completed his undergraduate and graduate work at the Chicago Conservatory of Music and Roosevelt University. After college, Richard became a print arranger for Hansen Publications and later became music director of Columbia Pictures Publications. In 1977, he co-founded his own publishing company, Bradley Publications, which is now exclusively distributed worldwide by Warner Bros. Publications.

Richard is equally well known for his piano workshops, clinics, and teacher training seminars. He was a panelist for the first and second Keyboard Teachers' National Video Conferences, which were attended by more than 20,000 piano teachers throughout the United States.

The home video version of his adult teaching method, How to Play Piano With Richard Bradley, was nominated for an American Video Award as Best Music Instruction Video, and, with sales climbing each year since its release, it has brought thousands of adults to—or back to—piano lessons. Still, Richard advises, "The video can only get an adult started and show them what they can do. As they advance, all students need direct input from an accomplished teacher."

Additional Richard Bradley videos aimed at other than the beginning pianist include How to Play Blues Piano and How to Play Jazz Piano. As a frequent television talk show guest on the subject of music education, Richard's many appearances include "Hour Magazine" with Gary Collins, "The Today Show," and "Mother's Day" with former "Good Morning America" host Joan Lunden, as well as dozens of local shows.

Project Manager: Zobeida Pérez
Art Design: María A. Chenique

BRADLEY™ is a trademark of Warner Bros. Publications

Contents

All I Want for Christmas Is My Two Front Teeth 60

Away in a Manger...36

Blue Christmas 76

Christmas Lullaby 44

Deck the Halls...66

Don't Save It All for Christmas Day 39

The First Noel 17

Frosty the Snowman 6

Grown-Up Christmas List...20

Hark! The Herald Angels Sing...82

Have Yourself a Merry Little Christmas...3

(There's No Place Like) Home for the Holidays...94

I'll Be Home for Christmas...91

Jingle Bells 46

Joy to the World...32

Let It Snow! Let It Snow! Let It Snow!...51

The Little Drummer Boy...10

Nuttin' for Christmas...73

O Christmas Tree (O Tannenbaum)...79

O Come, All Ye Faithful...63

O Little Town of Bethlehem...88

Santa Claus Is Comin' to Town...70

Silent Night...14

Star of the East...86

Suzy Snowflake...25

The Twelve Days of Christmas...28

Winter Wonderland 48

You're a Mean One, Mr. Grinch 54

Have Yourself a Merry Little Christmas

Words and Music by
HUGH MARTIN and RALPH BLANE
Arranged by Richard Bradley

4

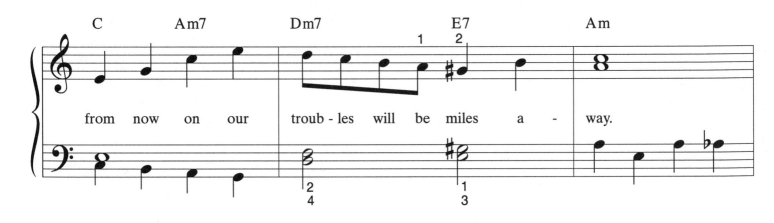

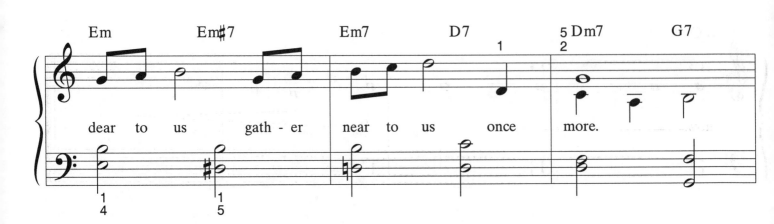

Frosty the Snowman

Words and Music by
STEVE NELSON and JACK ROLLINS
Arranged by Richard Bradley

Frosty the Snowman - 4 - 1

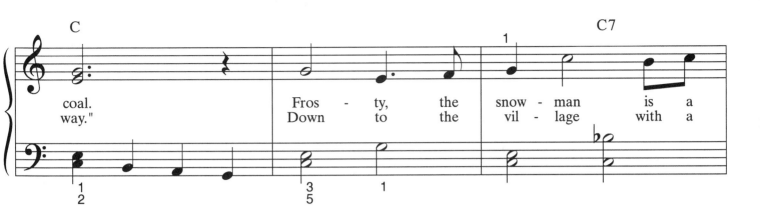

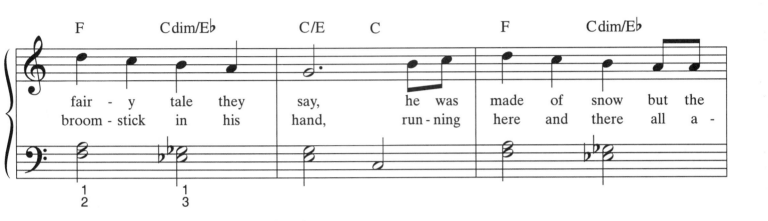

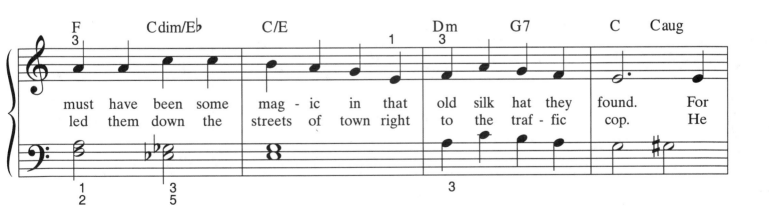

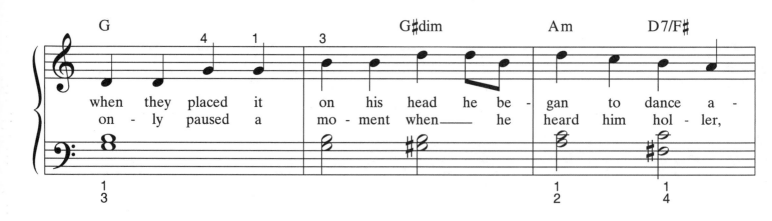

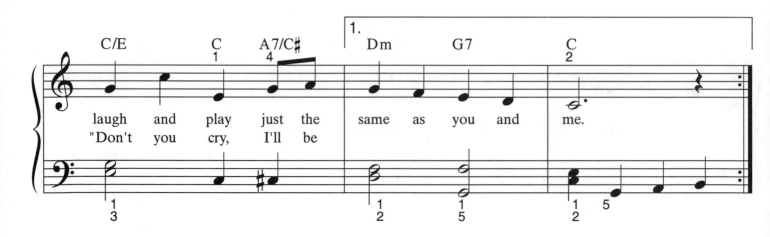

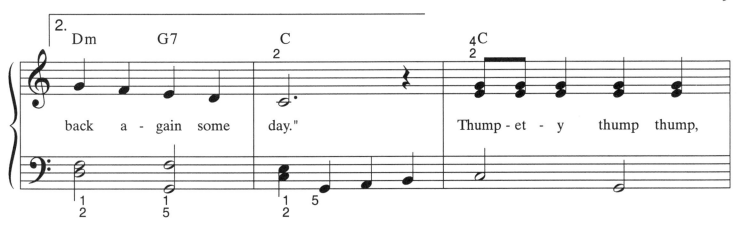

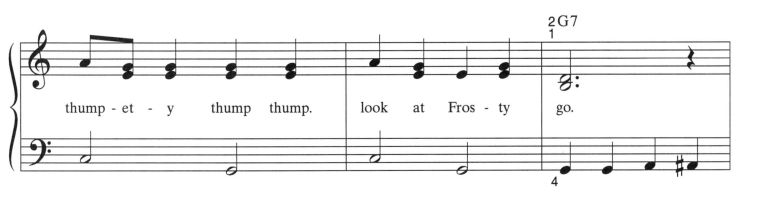

The Little Drummer Boy

Words and Music by
KATHERINE DAVIS, HENRY ONORATI
and HARRY SIMEONE
Arranged by Richard Bradley

The Little Drummer Boy - 4 - 1

Silent Night

Words by
JOSEPH MOHR

Music by
FRANZ GRUBER
Arranged by Richard Bradley

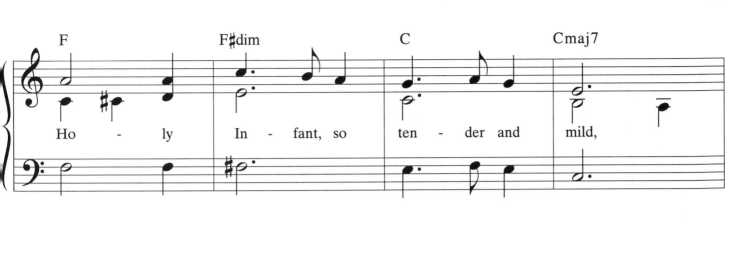

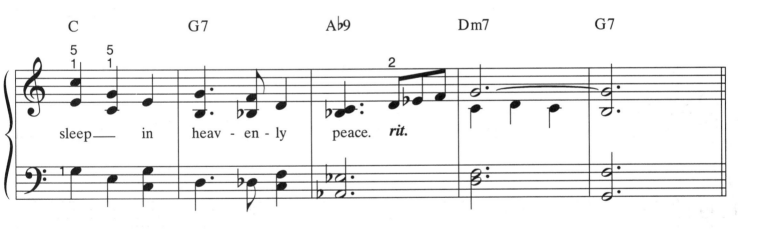

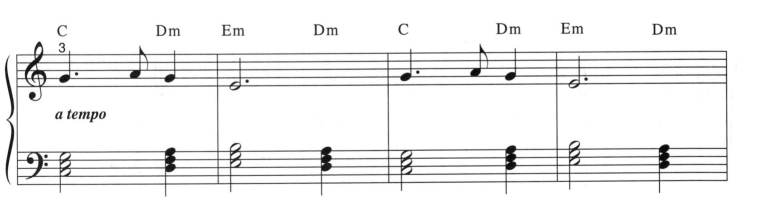

The First Noel

TRADITIONAL
Arranged by Richard Bradley

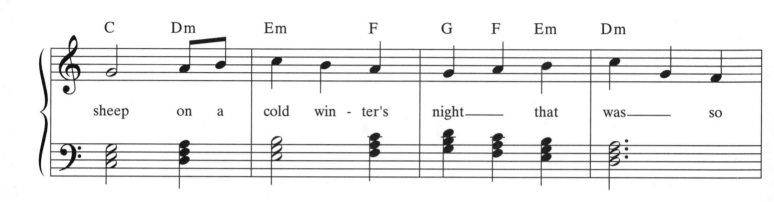

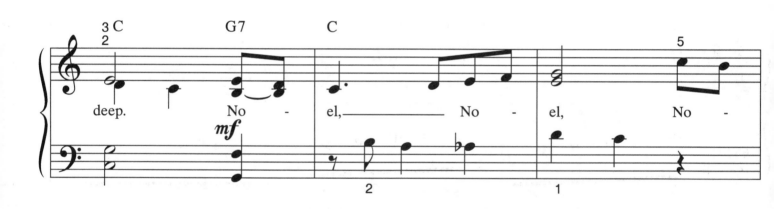

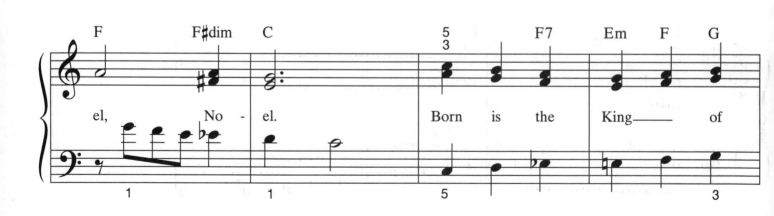

Grown-Up Christmas List

Words and Music by
DAVID FOSTER and LINDA THOMPSON JENNER
Arranged by Richard Bradley

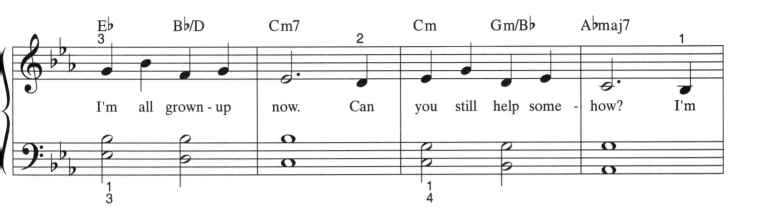

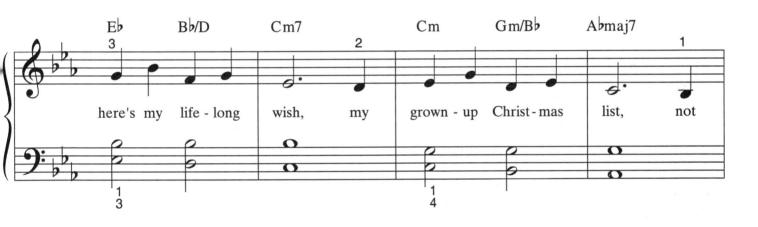

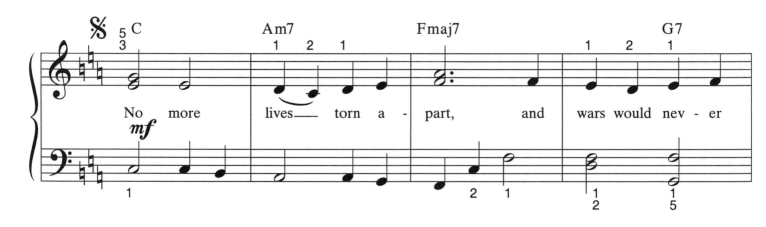

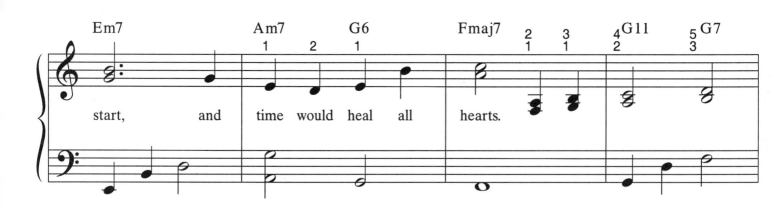

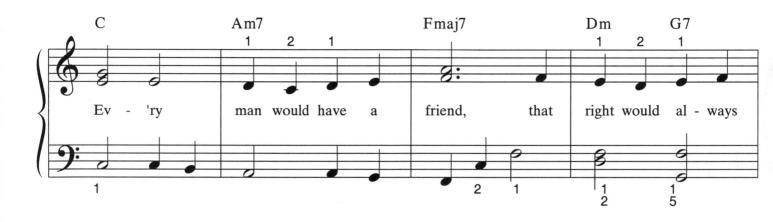

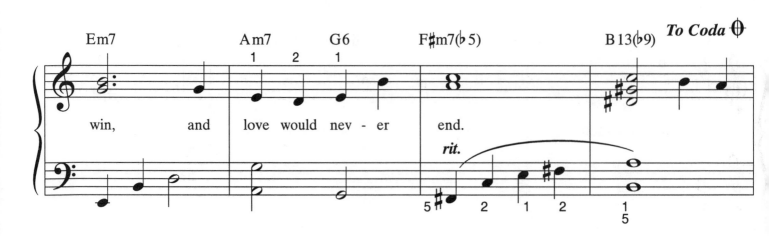

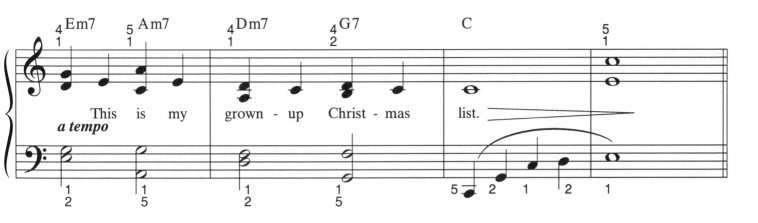

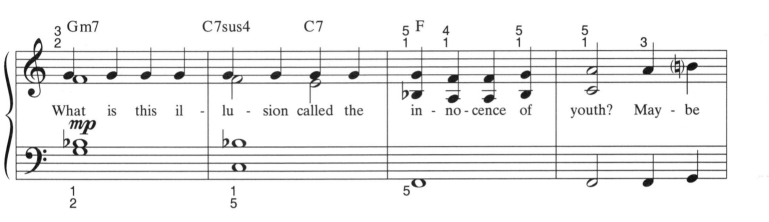

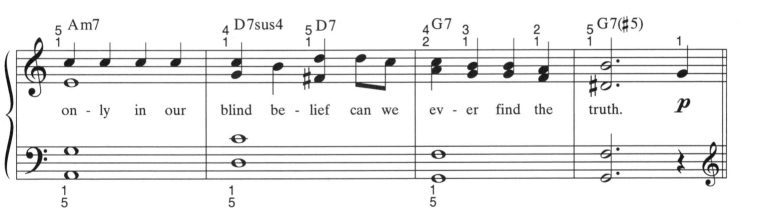

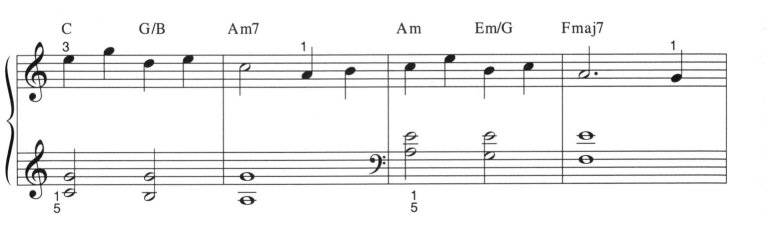

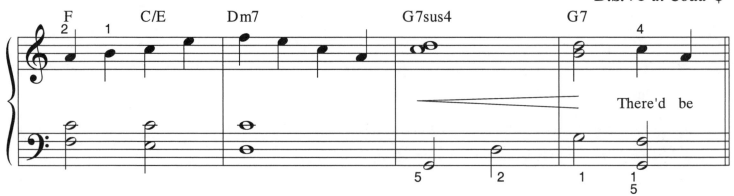

Coda

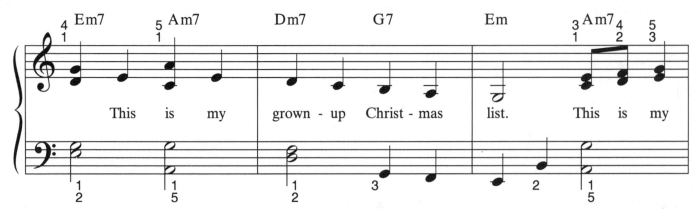

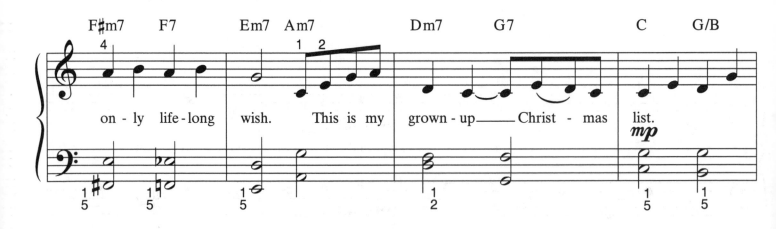

Suzy Snowflake

Words and Music by
SID TEPPER and **ROY BRODSKY**
Arranged by Richard Bradley

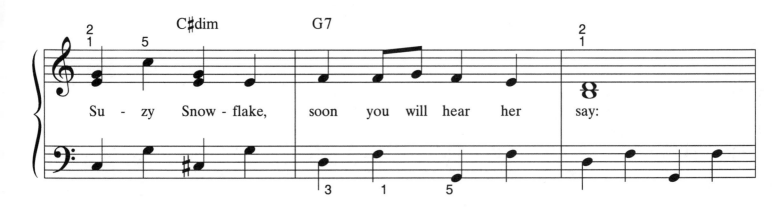

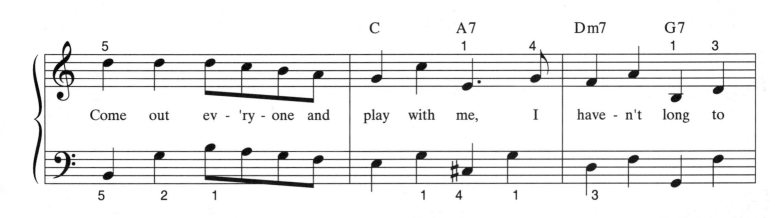

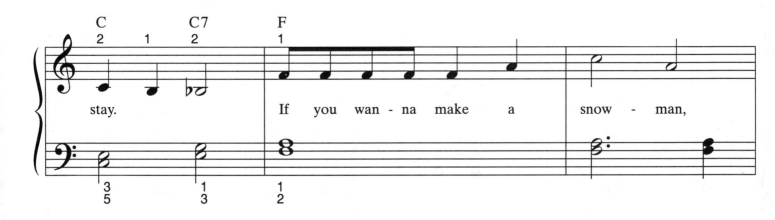

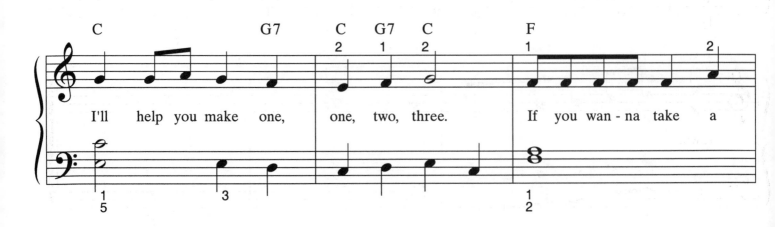

The Twelve Days of Christmas

TRADITIONAL
Arranged by Richard Bradley

The Twelve Days of Christmas - 4 - 1

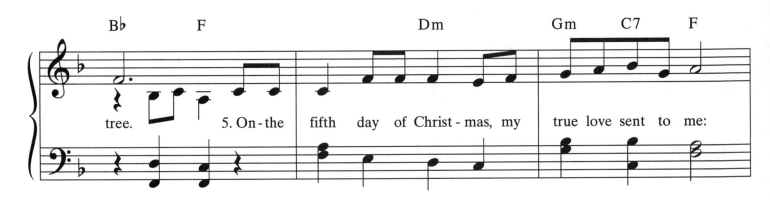

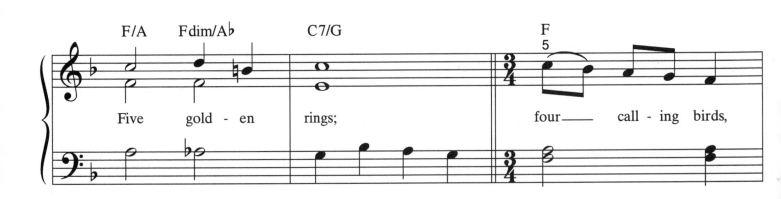

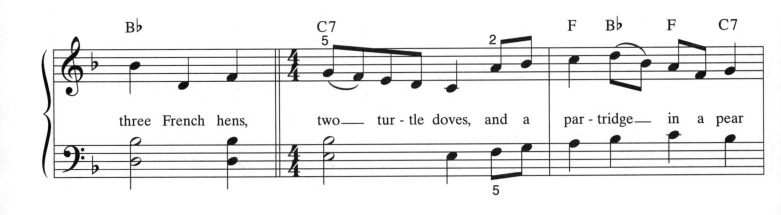

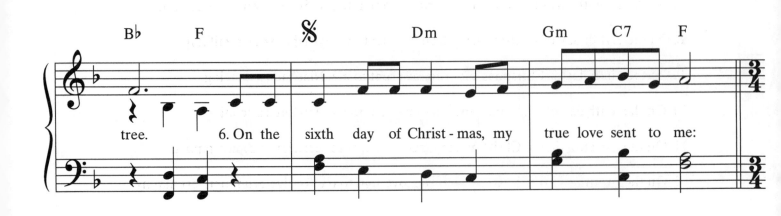

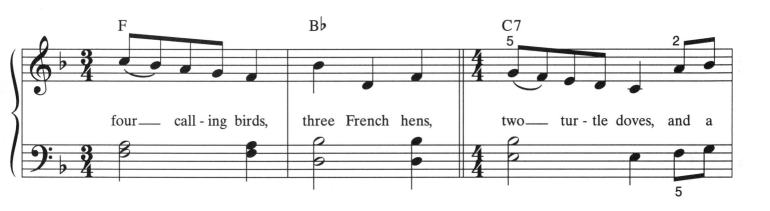

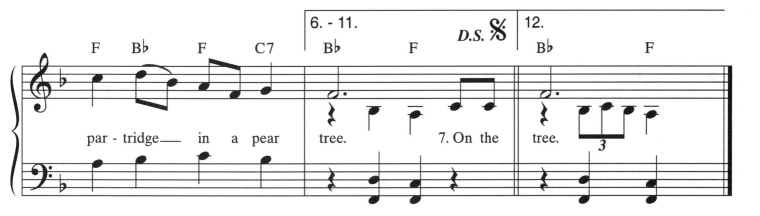

7. On the seventh day of Christmas, my true love sent to me: Seven swans a-swimming,

8. On the eighth day of Christmas, my true love sent to me: Eight maids a-milking,

9. On the ninth day of Christmas, my true love sent to me: Nine ladies dancing,

10. On the tenth day of Christmas, my true love sent to me: Ten lords a-leaping,

11. On the eleventh day of Christmas, my true love sent to me: Eleven pipers piping,

12. On the twelfth day of Christmas, my true love sent to me: Twelve drummers drumming,

Joy to the World

By ISSAC WATTS and
GEORGE FREDERICK HANDEL
Arranged by Richard Bradley

34

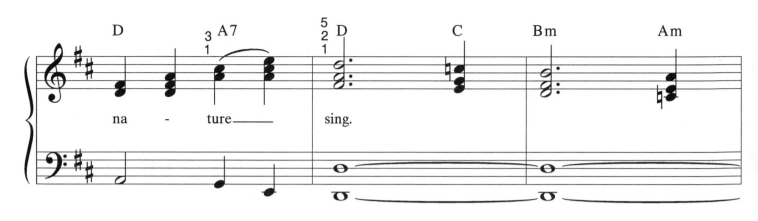

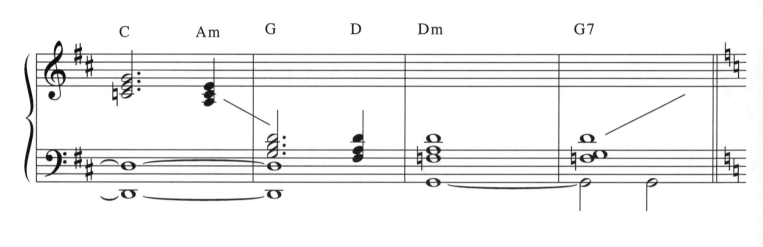

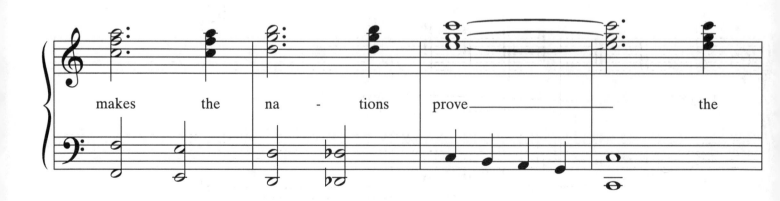

Away in a Manger

By
JAMES E. MURRAY
Arranged by Richard Bradley

Don't Save It All for Christmas Day

Words and Music by
PETER ZIZZO, RIC WAKE and CELINE DION
Arranged by Richard Bradley

Don't get so bus-y that you miss giv-ing just a lit-tle kiss

Don't Save It All for Christmas Day - 5 - 1

Verse 2:
How could you wait another minute,
A hug is warmer when you're in it.
And, baby, that's a fact.
And saying I love you's always better,
Seasons, reasons, they don't matter.
So don't hold back.
How many people in this world,
So needful in this world?
How many people are praying for love?
(To Chorus:)

Christmas Lullaby

Lyrics by
PEGGY LEE

Music by
CY COLEMAN
Arranged by Richard Bradley

Jingle Bells

Words and Music by
JOHN PIERPONT
Arranged by Richard Bradley

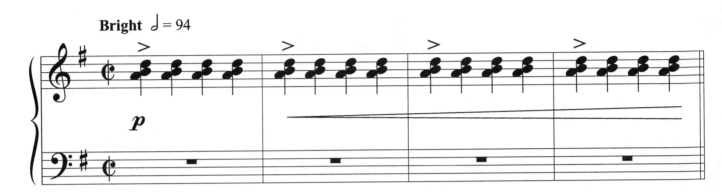

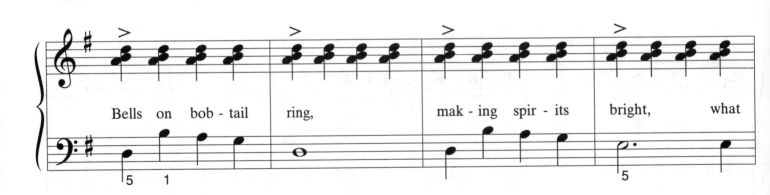

Winter Wonderland

Words by
DICK SMITH

Music by
FELIX BERNARD
Arranged by Richard Bradley

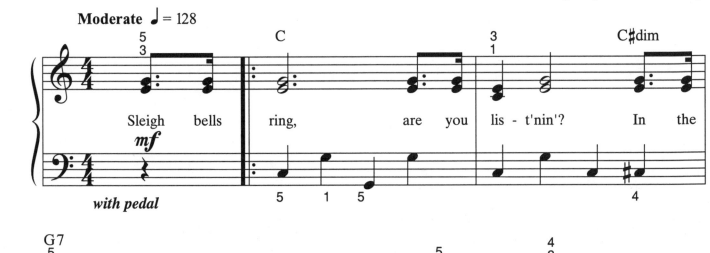

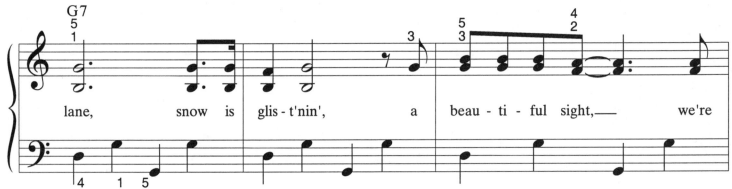

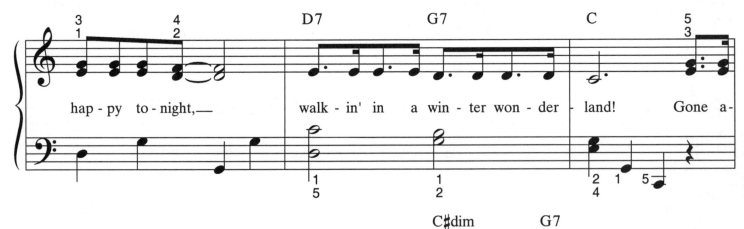

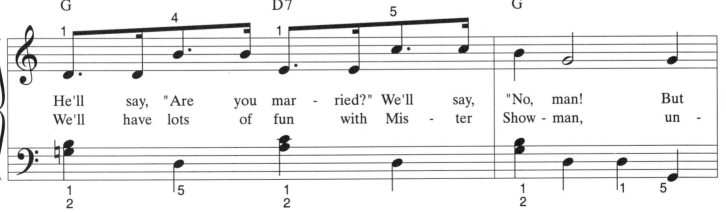

new bird. { He sings a love song.____ } as we go a - long,____
{ He's sing - ing a song,____ }

walk - in' in a win - ter won - der - land! In the mead - ow we can build a

snow - man, { then pre - tend that he is Par - son Brown.
{ and pre - tend that he's a cir - cus clown.

He'll say, "Are you mar - ried?" We'll say, "No, man! But
We'll have lots of fun with Mis - ter Show - man, un -

50

Let It Snow! Let It Snow! Let It Snow!

Words by
SAMMY CAHN

Music by
JULE STYNE
Arranged by Richard Bradley

Moderate ♩ = 112

mp

with pedal

mf

Oh! the weath-er out-side is fright-ful, but the

F/A Fdim/A♭ Gm7 C7 D7 Gm7 C7 D7

fire is so de-light-ful, and since we've no place to

Gm Fdim/A♭ Gm7 C7 F

go, Let it snow! Let it snow! Let it snow! It

Let It Snow! Let It Snow! Let It Snow! - 3 - 1

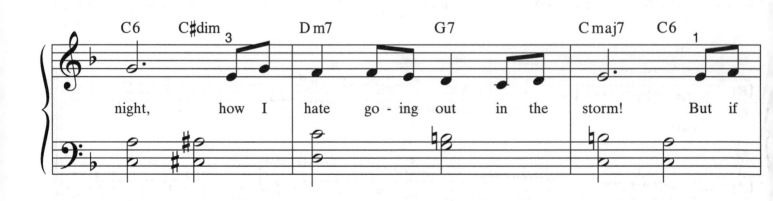

You're a Mean One, Mr. Grinch

From the Universal Motion Picture
Dr. Seuss' How the Grinch Stole Christmas

Lyrics by DR. SEUSS
Music by ALBERT HAGUE
Arranged by Richard Bradley

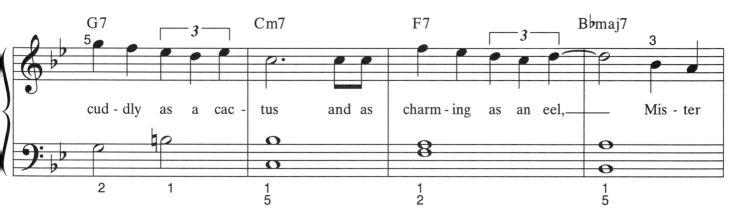

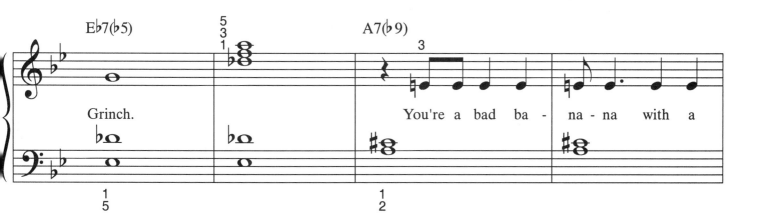

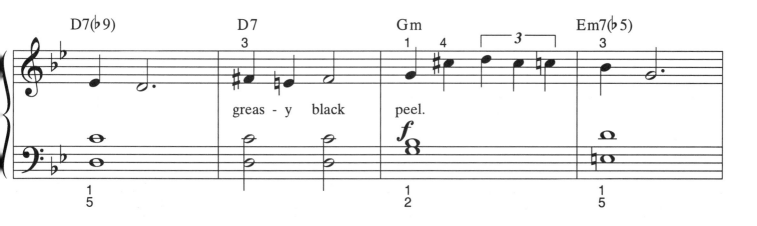

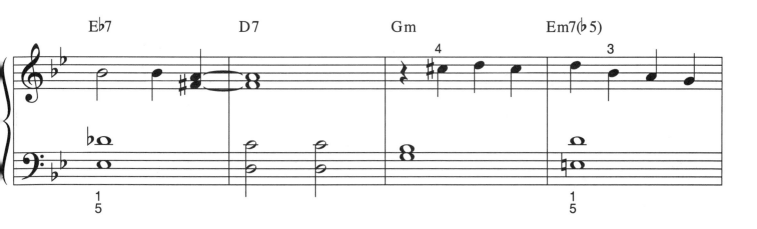

56

58

All I Want for Christmas Is My Two Front Teeth

Words and Music by
DON GARDNER
Arranged by Richard Bradley

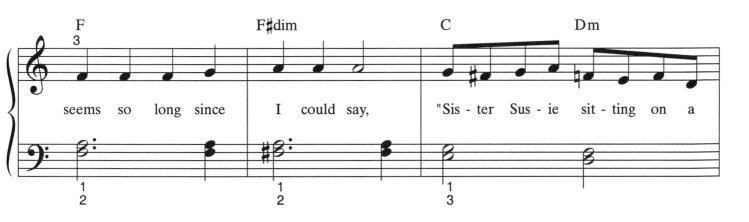

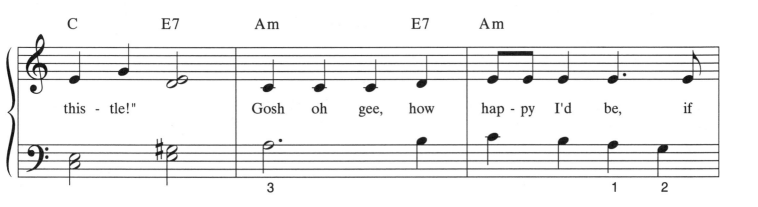

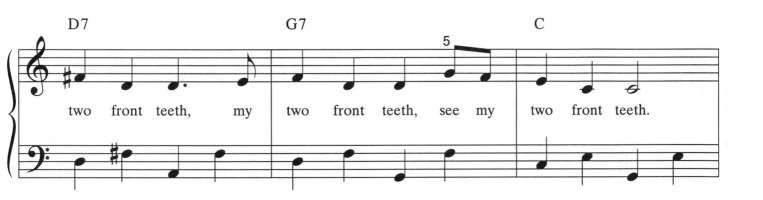

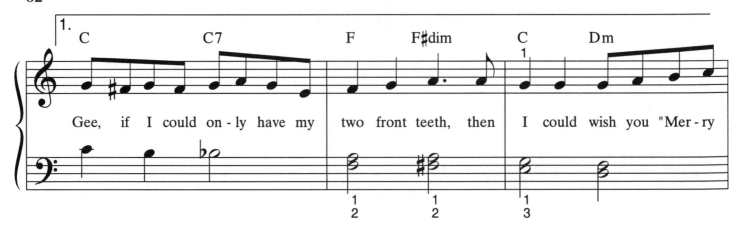

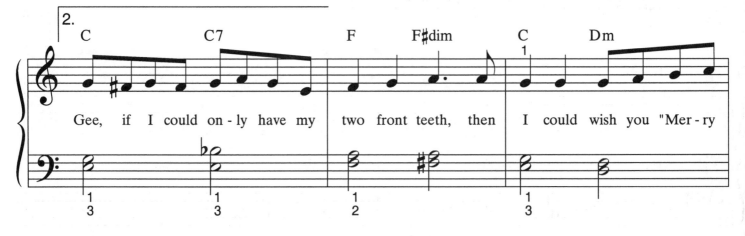

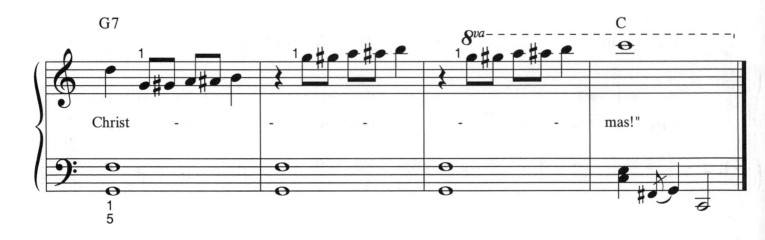

O Come, All Ye Faithful

TRADITIONAL
Arranged by Richard Bradley

64

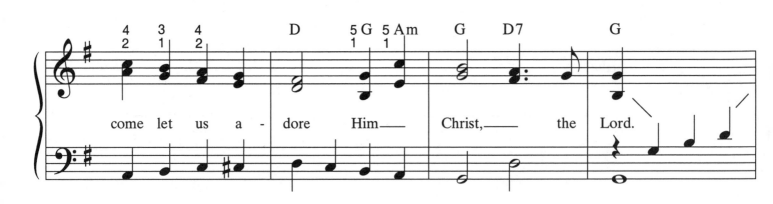

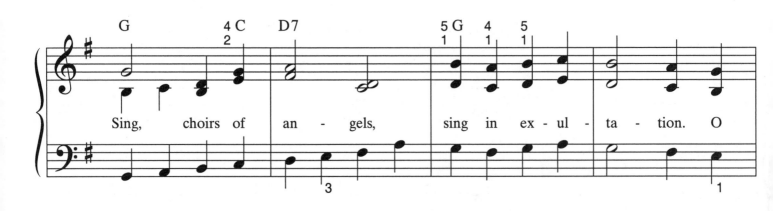

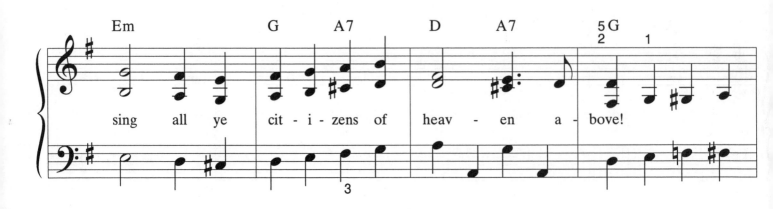

O Come, All Ye Faithful - 3 - 3

Deck the Halls

TRADITIONAL
Arranged by Richard Bradley

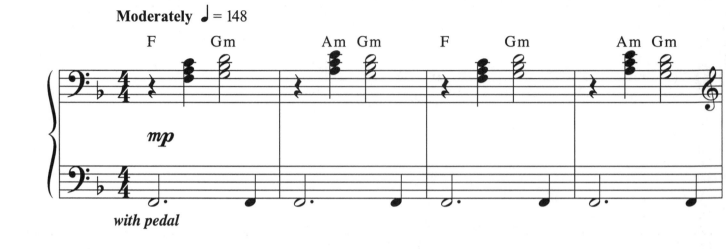

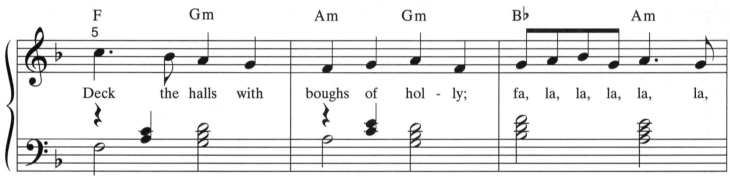

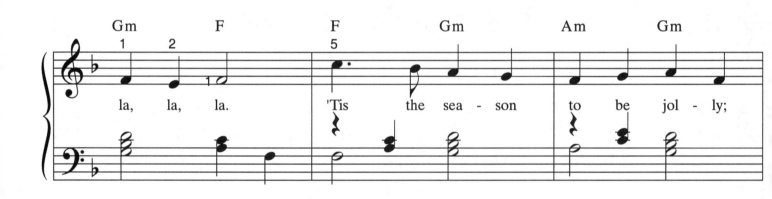

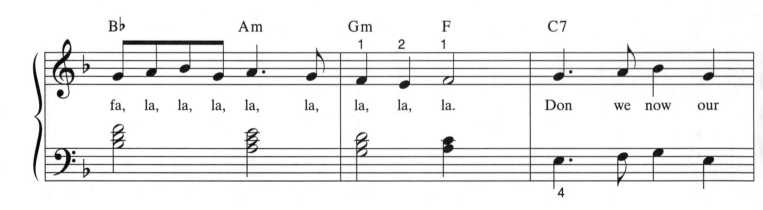

Deck the Halls - 4 - 1

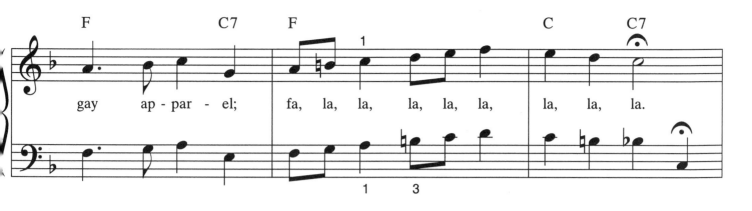

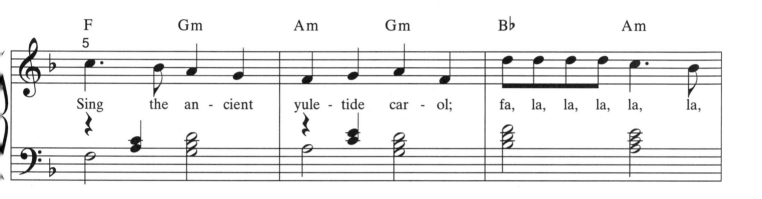

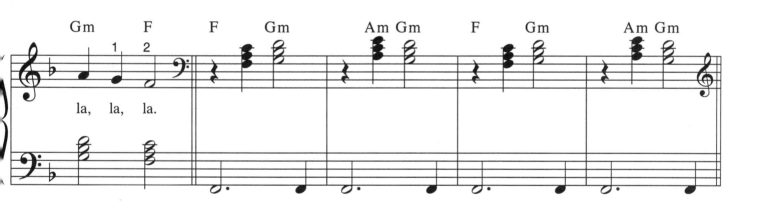

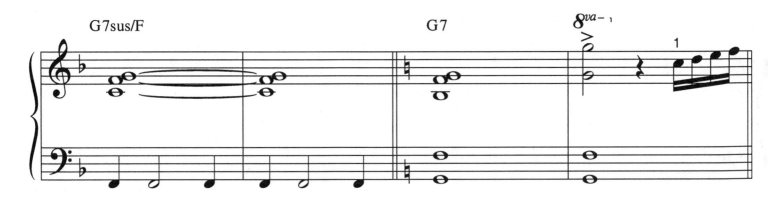

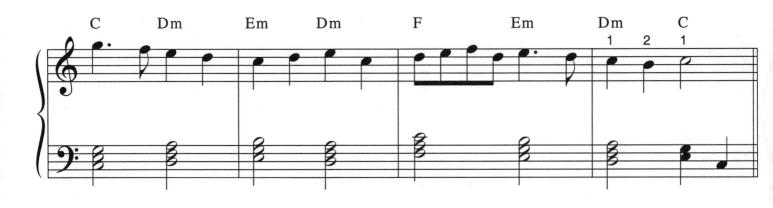

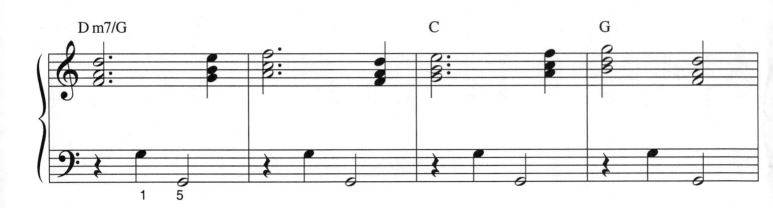

Santa Claus Is Comin' to Town

Words by
HAVEN GILLESPIE

Music by
J. FRED COOTS
Arranged by Richard Bradley

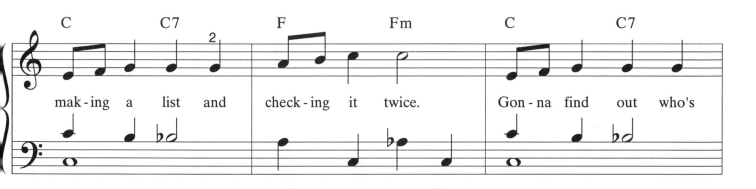

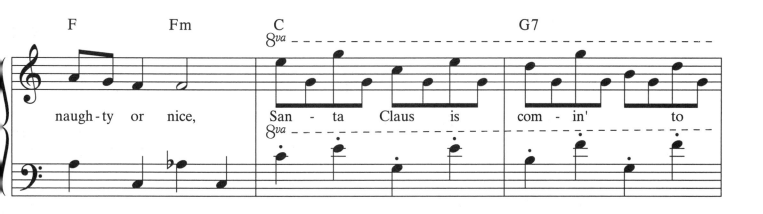

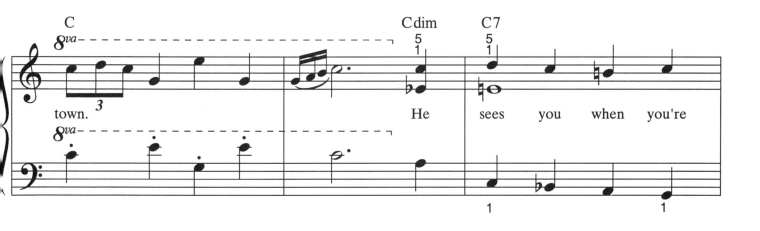

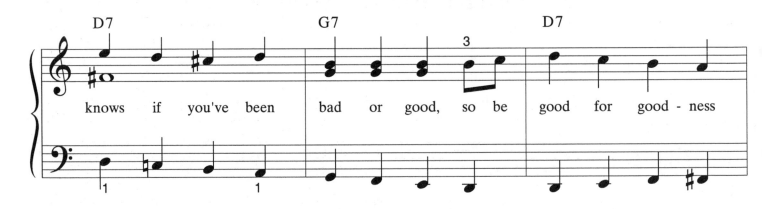

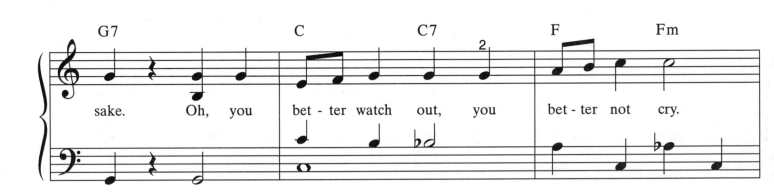

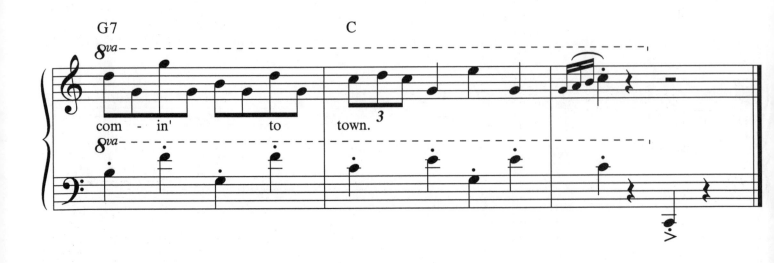

Nuttin' for Christmas

Words and Music by
SID TEPPER and ROY C. BENNETT
Arranged by Richard Bradley

74

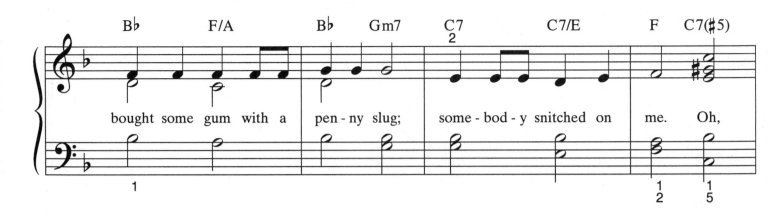

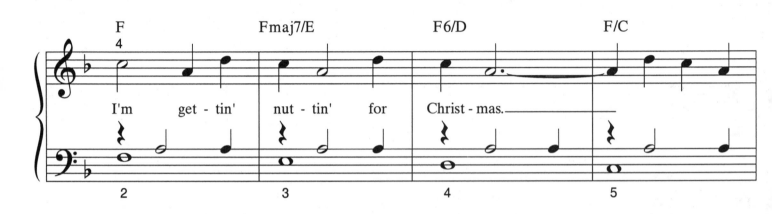

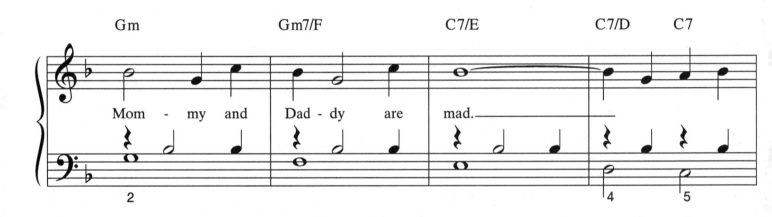

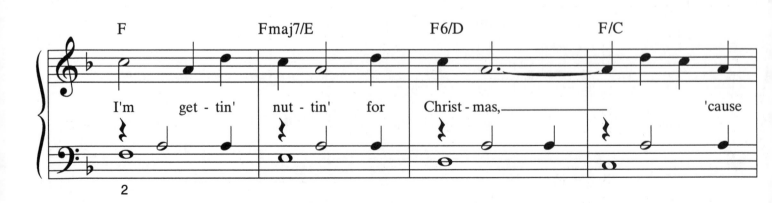

Verse 2:
I put a tack on teacher's chair; somebody snitched on me.
I tied a knot in Susie's hair; somebody snitched on me.
I did a dance on Mommy's plants; climbed a tree and tore my pants.
Filled the sugar bowl with ants; somebody snitched on me. So, . . .

Verse 3:
I won't be seeing Santa Claus; somebody snitched on me.
He won't come visit me because somebody snitched on me.
Next year I'll be going straight, next year I'll be good, just wait,
I'd start now but it's too late; somebody snitched on me. Oh, . . .

Blue Christmas

Words by
JAY W. JOHNSON

Music by
BILLY HAYES
Arranged by Richard Bradley

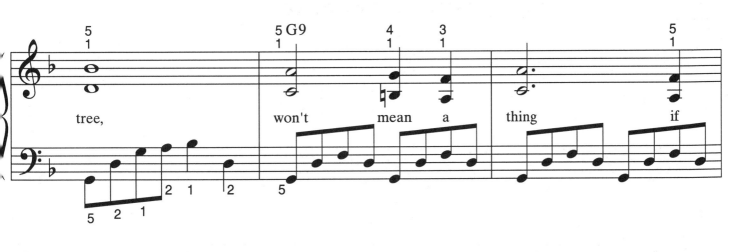

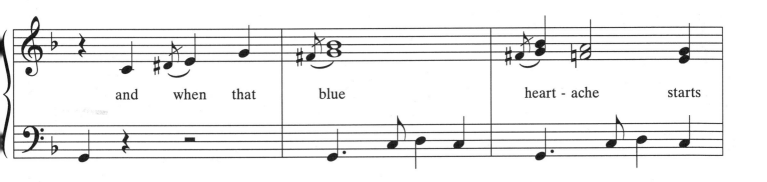

Blue Christmas - 3 - 2

78

O Christmas Tree
(O Tannenbaum)

GERMAN CAROL
Arranged by Richard Bradley

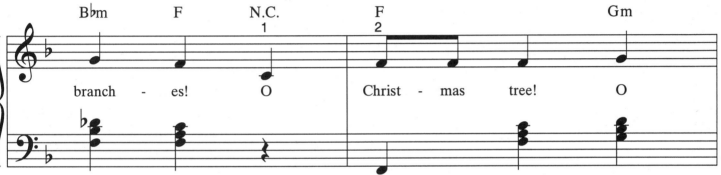

O Christmas Tree - 3 - 1

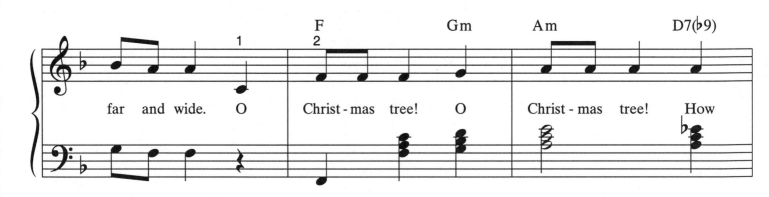

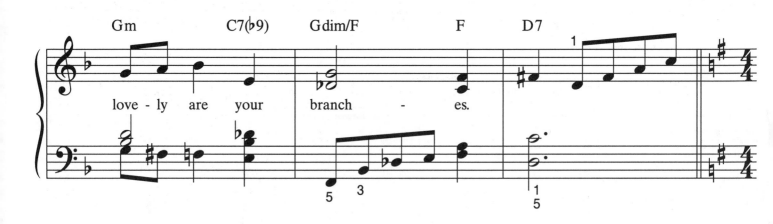

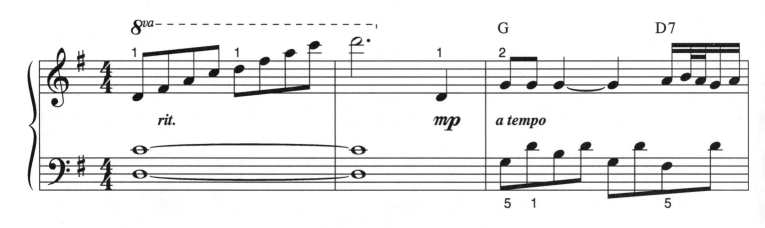

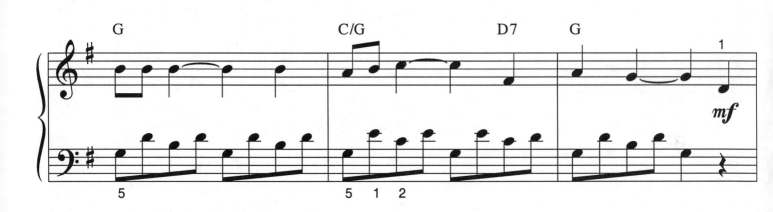

O Christmas Tree - 3 - 3

Hark! The Herald Angels Sing

Words by
CHARLES WESLEY

Music by
FELIX MENDELSSOHN
Arranged by Richard Bradley

84

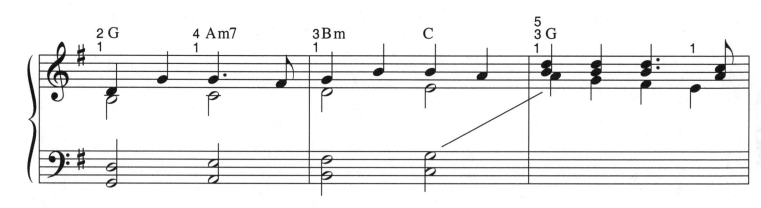

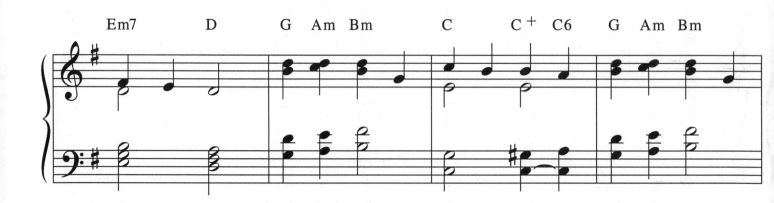

Hark! The Herald Angels Sing - 4 - 3

Hark! The Herald Angels Sing - 4 - 4

Star of the East

Words by
GEORGE COOPER

Music by
AMANDA KENNEDY
Arranged by Richard Bradley

Star of the East - 2 - 2

O Little Town of Bethlehem

By
LEWIS H. REDNER
Arranged by Richard Bradley

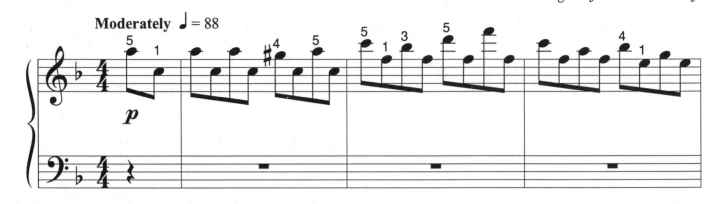

with pedal

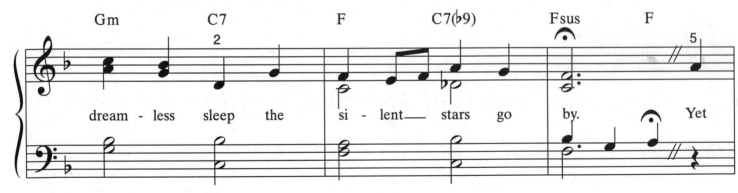

O Little Town of Bethlehem - 3 - 1

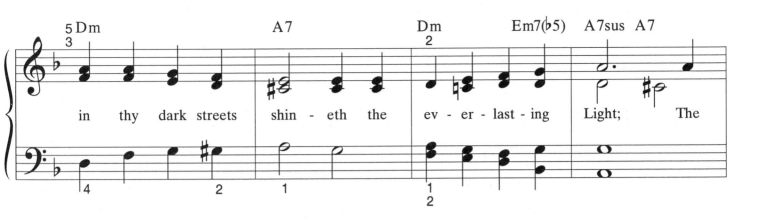

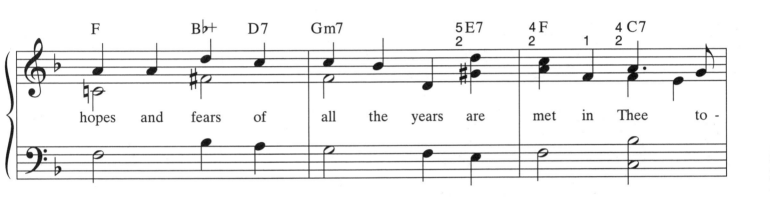

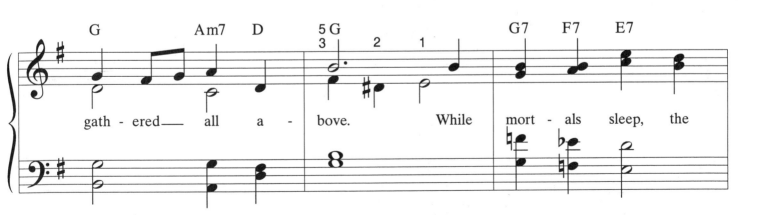

O Little Town of Bethlehem - 3 - 2

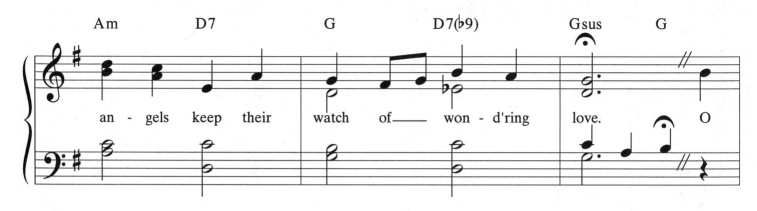

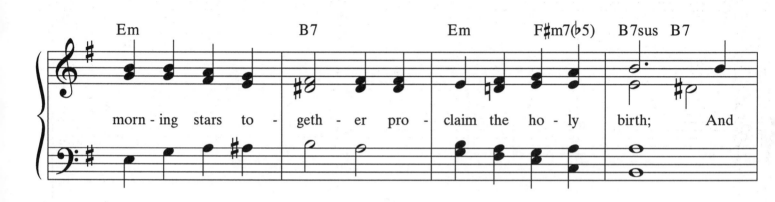

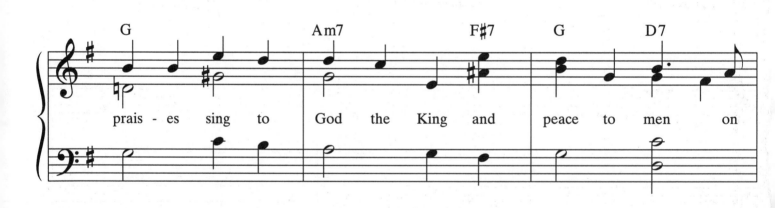

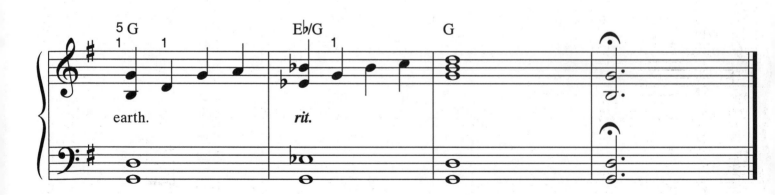

I'll Be Home for Christmas

Words by
KIM GANNON

Music by
WALTER KENT
Arranged by Richard Bradley

I'll Be Home for Christmas - 3 - 1

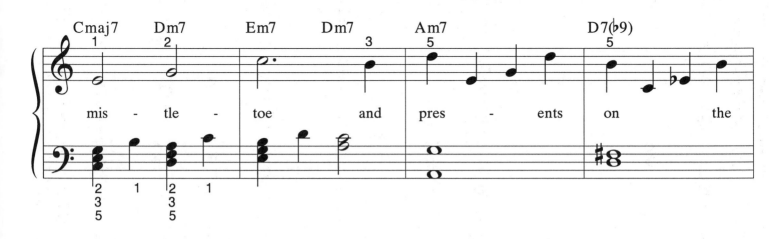

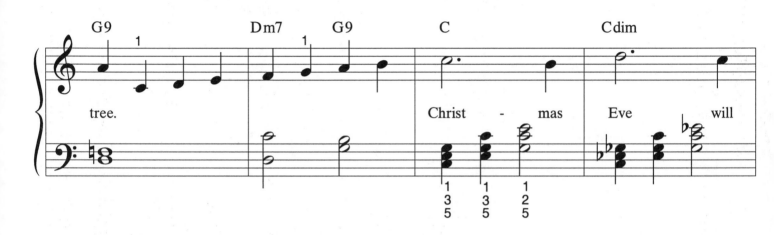

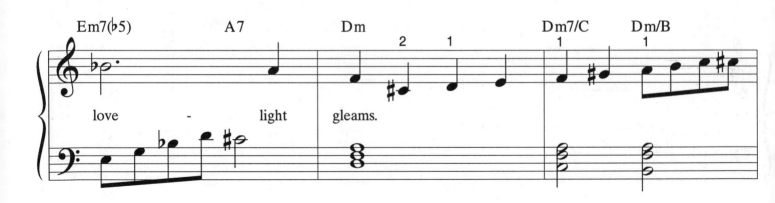

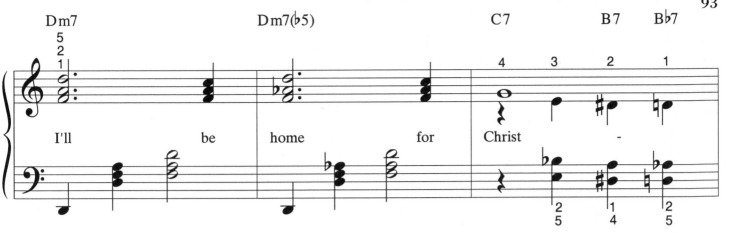

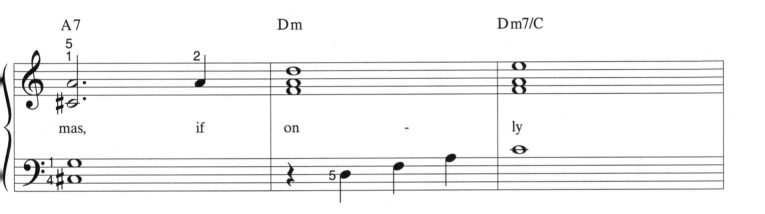

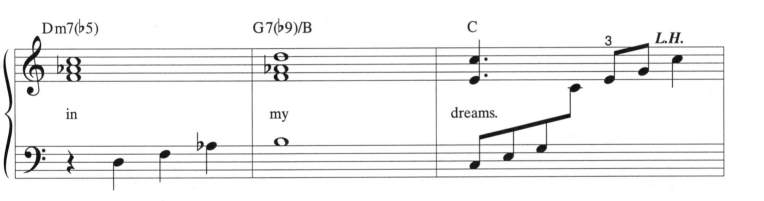

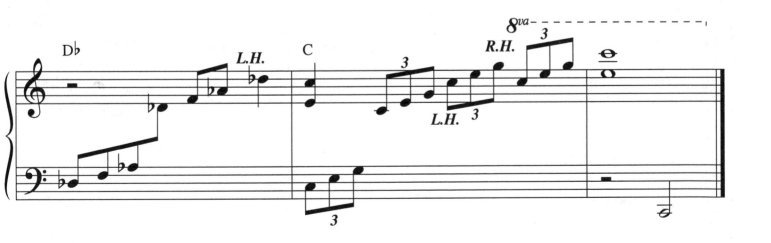

(There's No Place Like)
Home for the Holidays

Words by
AL STILLMAN

Music by
ROBERT ALLEN
Arranged by Richard Bradley

Home for the Holidays - 3 - 1

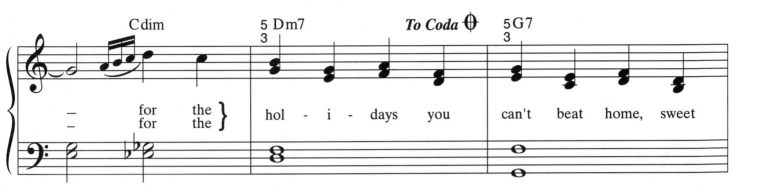

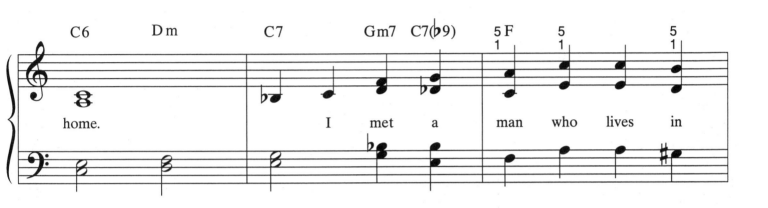

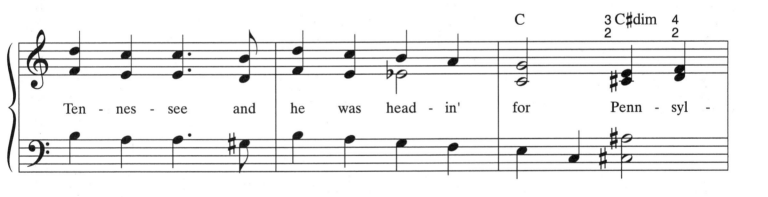

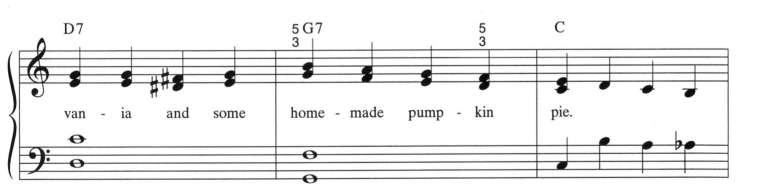